Endorsements

"In *The Disciple*, author David Sawler tackles some of the most basic yet misunderstood fundamentals of the faith—and he does it in his usual raw, candid style. His transparency is disarming and challenging. It's enjoyable and easy to read, but it will mess with your head, going right to the core of who you are and how you respond to the clarion call of the teachings of Jesus. It's truly life-changing."

MARK GRIFFIN
Coaching, Consulting, Speaking - Leadership Training

"David has a passion for a generation that has walked away from the institutional church. He has asked the questions and is now reminding the local church of its simple call to discipleship, which is the missing aspect in the church today. Dave speaks not only with authority and passion on the subject of discipleship, but also with humility. In this book,

David displays his heart for people and gives us practical
steps to jumpstart the church back to a discipleship lifestyle.
You will be challenged!"

GERRY MICHALSKI
Lead Pastor of Soul Sanctuary

"With all the deconstruction in books today, it is great to
read a book that builds some structure of what we can prac-
tically do in our faith journey to help disciple the generations below us."

BRETT ULLMAN
Executive Director: worldsapart.org

"In my travels, I am discovering a generation of young people who don't want to just hear about Jesus; they want to
live Him out in their day to day lives. The church does not
need a "walk away" generation; it needs a "reinvention" of
true discipleship. David Sawler removes the clutter and gets
us back to the biblical heartbeat of what it means to be a
disciple of Jesus Christ."

DON MANN
Founder of www.reinventingthechurch.com

"One of the most pressing issues to be addressed by the
Church in North America is that of making disciples of
Christ—not just converts, but fully formed followers of Jesus. Too many negative influences are making the status
quo unsustainable today. Dave Sawler has keen insight on
how to make the shifts necessary for newfound effective-

ness for leaders who are committed to obeying the command to 'make disciples.'"

GEORGE WERNER
Director, Mission Canada, Pentecostal Assemblies of Canada

"David is painfully hitting the spiritual nail on the head. The tedious and time-consuming journey of discipleship has been reduced to packages and programs. But there is hope. People like David are willing to commit themselves to this most rewarding and God-glorifying discipleship journey, which is the execution of the missionary mandate in its purest and most effective form."

JAN DEN OUDEN
Leader of Member Care, OM International

"David Sawler is a passionate practitioner of New Testament teaching. What you are about to read is the journey of a person who sees that the Bible and true biblical discipleship is not optional. It is critical to be a true follower of Jesus Christ. The refreshing approach is challenging and energizing. Read this book only if you are intent on being a follower of Jesus."

IAN GREEN
Visionary Leader, Next Level International & Proton Foundation

the disciple

GOD'S BLUEPRINT

DAVID SAWLER

THE DISCIPLE
God's Blueprint

ISBN-13: 978-1-77069-007-3

Printed by Word Alive Press
131 Cordite Road, Winnipeg, MB R3W 1S1
www.wordalivepress.ca

WORD ALIVE PRESS
Just Write!

To Matthew, Jordan,
and Amanda

Acknowledgements

There are many times that I have struggled to write and have a fresh word for those I am called to minister to. That was not the case with this project. While I have had the opportunity to write on other topics, this book is my heart.

I have had the incredible privilege of hearing and learning about discipleship from so many incredible men and women over the past two decades. This book is a result of all the powerful lessons which they have passed on. While, I know I am still on my journey to learning I am so thankful for what has already been passed on. To all those of you who have passed on your wisdom, I say thank you.

To my wife, Shirley, who has always supported, encouraged, and has put up with me during seasons of writing and business, I owe much gratitude. Also, to my children, Matthew, Jordan, and Amanda, who are my inspiration and reason for doing so much of what I do. While I hope others may benefit from the words in this book, my prayer is that my children will see and experience everything God has for them.

Also, thanks to all those who read, edited, gave input, and did so much work to make this project come together. Cathleen, Valerie, Rebecca, and Tim, it is greatly appreciated.

Lastly, I thank God for His grace, mercy, and willingness to use us in wonderful things He is doing today. Be blessed.

DAVE

Table of Contents

SECTION THREE

SECTION FOUR

1 FOREWORD

Foreword

I n most of the world, people are used to paying for movies, dinners, and sporting events, but usually not prayer
meetings. Several years ago while pastoring in Oakville,
just outside of Toronto in Canada, we held several prayer
events which actually did cost money to attend. These
events took place at the CN Tower, in the heart of the city,
which is one of the highest manmade structures in the
world. It cost quite a few dollars to take the elevator to the
observation decks near the top.

From the circular observation decks, we could see an
incredible distance in every direction. We would always do
this at night. The lights from thousands upon thousands of
buildings, cars, and homes were visible below us, right to
the horizon. Within our view, the nations of the world were
represented—as this is one of the most multicultural cities
in the world, with over one hundred languages spoken. It

was in this setting that I asked people to remember a day when Jesus also tried to teach his disciples an important lesson.

Jesus traveled through all the towns and villages of that area, teaching in the synagogues and announcing the Good News about the Kingdom. And he healed every kind of disease and illness. When he saw the crowds, he had compassion on them because they were confused and helpless, like sheep without a shepherd. He said to his disciples, *"The harvest is great, but the workers are few. So pray to the Lord who is in charge of the harvest; ask him to send more workers into his fields"* (Matthew 9:35-38, NLT)

From this vantage point, the view included millions upon millions of people. The number of people and issues represented in these lights were far beyond anything we were capable of dealing with. When we realized the spiritual need, it was simply overwhelming. We were left with the feeling, God, where do we even begin?

Over my lifetime, as I have prayed for my generation, I have been brought back to this scripture over and over again. We see Jesus moved with compassion when He tells His disciples, "Look, open your eyes, the 'Harvest is Great.'" It is like He is saying, "See those I love, see the ones for whom I will lay down my life, see the ones for whom the Father has sent Me." He is asking them to look and gain the same burden and compassion for those who are lost, wandering, confused, and hurting.

When we are hit with such a huge burden for our family, community, or country, it can simply be too much. I am sure the disciples were experiencing a similar moment as Jesus was teaching them this lesson. We can see Jesus' compassion for the crowd by His response to them. He told his disciples to first pray that the Lord of the Harvest would send workers. The Church's first response has often been to pray for the Lost, but this is not Jesus' first instruction.

If we are going to see our nations changed in the last days, then it is here where we must also start. Today we still need God to raise up workers, to raise up those who will reach and disciple the masses.

After this, Jesus does something that, again, may not be our first or second response. He tells them to go, and He sends them out. Perhaps they were thinking, after His first instruction, that He was only speaking about other people. However, we see that this prayer included them. When we pray that God will send workers, the prayer must include, "Father, please raise me up."

My prayer for you, as you read this book, is that you will be challenged as to what a disciple of Christ looks like. From the lessons Jesus left us, we will present a new, yet old, definition for this life we are called to live.

This book certainly does not present a new discipleship program, nor will living out what is written in this book be something you will be able to add to what you are already doing. Taking on the challenges that are written about here may mean revolutionizing the idea of what following Jesus is really all about.

I would ask you to begin this journey by doing something very simple, yet dangerous. Ask God to open your eyes to see the life of Jesus in a brand new way, and to re-imagine what following Him even looks like. Ask Him to let you be overwhelmed, like our prayer group was as we saw countless millions of people from the top of the CN Tower. Then ask yourself, "Father, whatever you need to do in me to live out my calling to reach and influence my generation please, do it in me."

IDEA

Overlooking

Some things are better experienced than simply explained. Instead of just hearing the stories mentioned in this book, I am encouraging you to try and put yourself into the story. Why not try having an experience like the one that is mentioned in Matthew 9:35-38? Or perhaps one like our prayer group had at the CN Tower many years ago.

Go somewhere where you can see many people—a mall, a sporting event, a concert, or a hillside overlooking your community. Take a few moments and just sit there and open your eyes. While you are seeing the multitudes, ask God to fill you with compassion for them. Ask that you would begin to experience the same burdens that He does. From this vantage point, pray that God would send and raise up workers to your harvest field. But remember, pray that God would begin with you

2 INTRO

Intro

Many times, over the course of my life, I have been challenged to share the Gospel with those who have never heard it. I have taken part in countless events and outreaches out of a sincere desire to share the Good News with friends, family, and others. I have travelled around the world doing missions work. Presently, I am working with a church planting ministry in Nova Scotia, Canada.

Likely, you are one of the millions of people, from all over the world, who are living out your faith just like me— people called by God, people giving their best effort and sincerely trying to live out the commission that Jesus left with us.

What is hard to believe is that, despite our good intentions, the church in the western world is simply not growing. In fact, most mainline denominations are, or will be, struggling for their own existence. Despite our honest effort, time, money, prayer, work, events, programs, websites, podcasts, and radio and TV evangelists, it has been said that only one percent of church growth in North America is non-biological. This means that the majority of church growth is coming from children being born into the faith. We are seeing very few lasting results for the amount of seed that has been sown.

So many people and ministries have tried almost everything to be relevant and fruitful in their locations. They have used new and old methods, schemes, contemporary services, traditional services, and new church models… and have spent millions of dollars doing it. However, the results have not even been close to what they were expecting.

It has left so many people discouraged and wondering, *Is it supposed to be this difficult?* Why would Jesus leave us a mission that was so extremely difficult, or perhaps one that wouldn't work at all? After putting so much effort into initiatives that produce so few lasting results, many individuals are left believing they will never see their own family, church, or community transformed. Many are left thinking, *I guess this is as good as it is going to get.*

From the story of the sower in Luke, we know that all the seed that is sown won't last or take root. However, shouldn't we be expecting more? What about the crop that is supposed to increase one hundred fold? Can we believe that is possible and really ever see it happen?

> *"'Still other seed fell on fertile soil. This seed grew and produced a crop that was a hundred times as much as had been planted!' When he had said this, he called out, 'Anyone with ears to hear should listen and understand.'"*
>
> (Luke 8:8, NLT)

I still believe He is *"not wanting anyone to perish, but everyone to come to repentance"* (2 Peter 3:9, NIV). I still believe it is actually possible that there is good soil that can produce a great harvest, even a hundred times more.

I believe that the commission Jesus gave to His disciples many years ago still stands for us today.

> *"I have been given all authority in heaven and on earth. Therefore, go and make disciples of all the nations, baptizing them in the name of the Father and the Son and the Holy Spirit. Teach these new disciples to obey all the commands I have given you. And be sure of this: I am with you always, even to the end of the age."*
>
> (Matthew 28:18-20, NLT)

We may be familiar with the Great Commission. But if we are not seeing it work, then perhaps we have missed the point of these words. Maybe the answer to why we are not seeing a great harvest is so simple and costly that we have missed it, perhaps even on purpose.

As you read the following chapters, I would ask that you try to wipe the slate clean. I have often wondered what the church today would look like if we didn't have our own preconceived ideas of what it should look like, or what discipleship should look like. Would things look different if we could start over without all the clutter? This is where the challenge starts for each one of us. Can we move forward while holding onto so much? At times, we need to let go of the good things we have in order to really grasp God's best for us.

This book does not promote any one discipleship structure. There are many incredible models that are being used in different churches around the world. Every one of them may look different, but at their core you will find many common principles. That is where this book will focus.

SECTION
ONE

3 JESUS IS THE MODEL, JESUS THE DISCIPLE + +

Jesus Is the Model,
Jesus the Disciple

Giving away the ending of a book at the beginning is something you never want to do. However, the following chapters cannot be correctly understood without the subsequent foundation. Everything in this book is based on two simple truths that I believe. First, the life of Jesus is God's blueprint for producing lasting fruit. Second, Jesus is the model of what a disciple is. While they might not seem to be earth-shattering at first glance, their implications can change everything we do as followers of Jesus.

Let's start at the actual source: Jesus. We can read about His life throughout the Gospels and yet miss the obvious. It was through His life, death, and resurrection that salvation was bought and paid for. We can look at His character and we can strive to become like Him. We can look at His works and pray that God uses us in similar and even greater ways.

We can know all of these things and still miss some-thing. Many people throughout the course of history have searched diligently and looked for a new or secret method to reaching their own generation. They have desperately sought after fruitfulness.

Jesus' life on earth was lived out by performing the will of the Father. Jesus' life is the Father's Blueprint for sharing the Good News with the world. Jesus' actions—what He did, where He went, who He hung out with—is the picture of God's perfect plan for producing true and lasting fruitful-ness.

The second foundation is this: Jesus is our model for what it means to be a disciple. Most teaching on disciple-ship focuses on Jesus as the teacher or Rabbi, but the Bible goes far beyond these limits. Throughout His life on earth, Jesus modelled what being a disciple truly entails.

For example, Jesus didn't simply teach the disciples how to pray by giving instruction though the Lord's Prayer. He went and prayed; He took time and they prayed together. He sent his disciples out to proclaim the Good News, but He proclaimed the Good News. He spoke and taught about serving, and He washed their feet.

Perhaps one of the greatest examples Jesus gives us takes place the night before His crucifixion. It is seen when He prays, *"Father, if you are willing, please take this cup of suffering away from me. Yet I want your will to be done, not mine"* (Luke 22:42, NLT). Here we see Jesus, who when faced with taking up His cross, totally gives Himself to the will of the Father. We see Jesus Himself living out obedience, selflessness, and submission—all of which are things He said we should do if we are to be His disciples.

In Jesus, we see words and actions operating together. He is the Word. He lived what He spoke. What a beautiful picture it is when we read a scripture like Philippians 2:3-8, which says,

> "Don't be selfish; don't try to impress others. Be humble, thinking of others as better than yourselves. Don't look out only for your own interests, but take an interest in others, too.
>
> You must have the same attitude that Christ Jesus had.
>
> Though he was God, he did not think of equality with God as something to cling to. Instead, he gave up his divine privileges; he took the humble position of a slave and was born as a human being. When he appeared in human form, he humbled himself in obedience to God and died a criminal's death on a cross."
>
> (NLT)

When we read the gospels and listen to the words Jesus spoke, we realize that what He was telling people to do, He had already done Himself. He calls each one of us to be a disciple, to disciple others, but all of this can only happen when we begin to be transformed into His likeness. He is the example.

> *"Let us fix our eyes on Jesus, the author and perfecter of our faith, who for the joy set before him endured the cross, scorning its shame, and sat down at the right hand of the throne of God."*
>
> (Hebrews 12:2, NIV)

4 WHO IS MY DISCIPLE?

+ + + +

Who Is My Disciple?

Recently, a pastor told me about a difficult time his church had gone through. A large portion of the members of his church had left after a series of difficult situations. After the dust settled, they made a remarkable discovery. They'd had several hundred people in intentional discipleship groups before the problems began. While a huge portion of the people in the church had left, the numbers of those in the discipleship groups remained almost the same. There is certainly a lesson to be learned here.

When we look at the birth of the Church in Acts, we see something similar. Just weeks and months earlier, Jesus is speaking to huge crowds. He is being followed daily, and the sick are being brought to him. Miracles are happening. The dead are being raised. Jesus is feeding thousands and walking on water. There is excitement in the air. There are people talking about what is happening. There is momentum.

Now Jesus has been crucified, has risen again, and has ascended into heaven. Some of the same people who months earlier had been fed by Jesus now yelled, "Crucify him!" Unlike the day of the sermon on the mount, it was now dangerous to associated with Christ. It is here where the scene of the Upper Room takes place, where the Holy Spirit is poured out. It is recorded that there were only one hundred and twenty people there.

Let's take a moment to consider who they were. Besides Judas, all of the disciples were there. Perhaps many of the seventy-two were there, too. It can certainly be argued that most of them would have been the people close to Jesus. When the going gets tough, it is disciples who are most likely to remain.

After spending many years sharing about why people leave the church, I have come to some conclusions. I now believe that knowing what discipleship is, and how to do it, may be the Church's biggest weakness today. What is astonishing about even making such a statement is that this is the mission and calling of the Church.

One of the things Jesus was called was "Truth." He spoke the Truth and was the true and living Word at the same time. In Jesus, we see what happens when someone actually lives what they say and believe. He spoke about fruitfulness and, at the same time, His life started something that has spread across an entire planet and outlasted every mocker, critic, and adversary.

Jesus lived out in the flesh what He is asking us to do. Consider this. After Jesus washed His disciples' feet, He said to them, *"I have given you an example to follow. Do as I have done to you"* (John 13:15, NLT). How did they understand that? Much of the teaching on this, and scriptures like it, focus on performing miracles like Jesus, about having the character of Christ, and on doing His good works. However, we may be missing the simplest answer of all, since it doesn't fit our Christian model.

Remember that this statement was spoken within the context of the twelve disciples, those closest to him. I believe they would have understood it as, "What I have just done, you now do." This is the same message Jesus repeats many times. For example, He says in John 15:9-10,

"As the Father has loved me, so have I loved you. Now remain in my love. If you obey my commands, you will remain in my love, just as I have obeyed my Father's commands and remain in his love" (NIV). This is something that is at the root of true discipleship: Christ likeness.

Jesus was telling His disciples to do for others what He had just done for them. Christ likeness does not just include character; it also includes deeds and actions. It is everything, your entire life. We may be guilty of trying to take parts of who Jesus is and living them out, but missing out on the one part He entrusted us with when He left, which is making disciples. It is here where we must be personally involved in the lives of others, where people have to actually know us.

Honestly, it scares us. This does not fit with a spectator-type church model where you can attend, but everyone remains at a safe distance.

While it is true that Jesus spoke to thousands of people, His main ministry was really to a select few. Take a moment to consider what the lives of the first disciples looked like. Jesus knew each of his disciples by name. Jesus knew who each of the twelve very personally. At the same time, if someone had asked one of the twelve disciples, "Who is your Rabbi?" or "Who are you following?", they undoubtedly would have said, "Jesus." There was a very specific relationship and no mistaking who Jesus called to follow him.

We may be failing to produce lasting disciples because, in our pride, we believed that we (whether you are a minister, church member, leader of some kind, or follower of Christ) could disciple an entire mass of people or congregation. It is true that we can teach, evangelize, and minister to many, much like Jesus did for the masses. However, perhaps it is impossible or unwise for one person to try and disciple so many people. Nowhere in Scripture are the crowds called disciples. We may be trying to do something that in His wisdom even Jesus wouldn't do.

The implication of believing that Jesus' life is God's blueprint for us totally changes what we do as believers. Our focus and goals change from just attending services or running programs to pouring our lives out for our friends. Have you ever pictured what your life would look like if you actually did what Jesus did on a daily basis? Spending time talking, praying, teaching, and encouraging others? Doing things that would even cause others religious people to call you a friend of sinners, glutton, or drunkard?

If we were literally following Jesus' model of discipleship, then someone could ask you, "Who is your disciple?" and you would be able to tell them who they are, by name. This would also mean that someone else could be asked who is helping and pouring into their life, and their answer would be your name. Surprisingly few people have fostered this kind of relationship, despite our declarations that making disciples is "our commission."

5 STOP PASSING THE BUCK

Stop Passing
the Buck

I f we are honest, most modern church models are set up in a such way that only a select few ever have the opportunity to take on ministry roles. Most Christians today have never actually been challenged, taught, or released to make disciples. However, all of Jesus' disciples—not just a few of them—were given the same commission (Matthew 28:18-20) Perhaps, if we are truly called to reach and disciple the masses, everyone will be needed and everyone will have a part.

Too often, Christians are put in church models where they are never asked to use their God-given gifts and responsibilities. They are asked to bring their friends to an event where someone else will share the Gospel with them. Then, they can send them to a class where someone else will teach them the basics of Christianity. Then, they can invite them to a church where they will receive teaching from a minister. In a sense, we can have church models that remove most of the congregation from being involved in the spiritual growth of others.

At the same time, we have to recognise that some people are gifted in specific areas. God raises up people who are incredible teachers. Others seem to have the ability to share their faith so easily. And on and on it goes. We must understand that the gifts of God are not just for the individual, but rather they are to bring maturity to the Church as a whole. If someone has the gifting of an evangelist, it is not simply meant to remain isolated with them. That person needs to help the body learn how to be evangelistic. One person's gifts must bring maturity and fruitfulness to the entire body.

The problem is that, when we take away a person's God-given responsibilities, we produce a generation void of real spiritual maturity. When we only teach people about discipleship, but do not allow them a venue to live it out, they become disillusioned and start to believe that it must only be meant for the select few. Like most things, the majority of us learn by doing. Teaching has its part, mentoring has its part, but nothing replaces lessons learned from first-hand experience. People have to be released to do what God has called them to do.

I have been told on several occasions that the longer someone attends church, the less likely they become to share their faith, bring someone to church, or have any non-

Christian friends. I have struggled with this, because I believe it should be the opposite. The truth is that you cannot become more like Jesus and become less fruitful. To grow spiritually, we must be becoming more and more like Jesus, the one who grew disciples. Perhaps we have missed the point on what maturity looks like by a lot.

The result of this model is something called Spectator Christianity. It is something you can watch, comment on, and critique without ever having to participate in it yourself. Spectator Christianity does not raise an army or movement. It does raise overweight, unmotivated, selfish, unhappy people with no real purpose. It is a model that only so many people can take part in. This leaves the majority of people feeling that if they can't sing or preach, they don't have any significant role in the Kingdom of God.

In most churches, only a small percentage of the people are involved with ministry, running programs, and even supporting financially. Perhaps there are reasons behind this—maybe in a traditional western church model we only need a small percentage active for our churches to operate. Maybe we don't really know what to do with everyone else anyway.

It is time that each of us took on what God has called us to do. In nature, a sign of maturity is the ability to reproduce. I think, in a spiritual sense, it goes even further. We must be able to reproduce our own kind. It is not enough that an apple tree can produce apples; it must produce apples with seeds that have the ability to produce a new tree, which will grow apples with seeds. If our spiritual lives don't operate the same way, we may produce some fruit, but not fruit that remains, as John 15:16 says we should.

Without a proper understanding of what our true calling is, we can fall into the trap where we want converts, but not disciples. This can even come out of a real desire to fulfil a God-given burden for lost people, but it is not all that God calls us to do. It is like we want to enjoy conception, because it is about the pleasure. However, that does not mean you want to raise kids.

It is unbelievable how much money is spent on evangelism, events, and outreaches. It is even more incredible how little lasting fruit we have from all our attempts at evangelism. While it is true that these things are necessary, perhaps at times our motivations are a bit off. It is astoundingly sad that a majority of our evangelism events somehow always involve us being in the limelight. Most of our evangelism events involve us being on a stage, us singing in front of people, us performing, us in the lights. We can be guilty of only being interested in sharing the Gospel if it is somehow about us. Too often, this is just a sign of the church's own selfish immaturity.

The truth is, we do need events, services, and outreaches. We need people to have real encounters with God, and someone does need to share the Gospel. We need people to come to repentance and be delivered from where they are into the Kingdom of God. But what needs to be learned is that conversion and discipleship only reach their full potential when accomplished together. Conversion without discipleship produces short-term results. Without conversion, you can't truly be discipled. It is through discipleship that you can experience life, fruitfulness, and a walk towards Christ likeness.

If you are going to see a great harvest today, you cannot simply pass on to others this responsibility to disciple. You have been called to disciple. You have not been called to simply invite people to church events. You have been called to get involved in the lives of others and lead them to Jesus. Ministers and pastors are not called to do this work for the church by themselves. According to Scripture, they are there to equip the church to do the work of the ministry. It is time to stop passing the buck and understand that it stops with you. Everyone is needed and everyone has a part.

IDEA

Balance

When we think of living a balanced life, we may think that sounds awfully boring. However, this may be one of the most radical things you ever do. The following is an exercise we did several years ago in one of the churches I pastored at. We were told to write down everything we did in a week related to the church, ministry, our faith, etc. While I recognize our whole lives are worship, for this exercise we broke our time down.

So I made my list of how many ministries I was involved with, who they were for, and how much time each one took. We were also challenged to think about how many of these ministries were to feed us spiritually, how many were for other believers, and how many were for those who did not know Christ.

I don't believe our results were much different than most other churches would have been. When I looked down at my own list of who most of the events were for, it made me think I must be terribly self-centered, and so is my church. Through this exercise, it was all too obvious that we were putting over ninety-nine percent of our efforts into feeding and taking care of our own. While these are things that must be done, we were terribly unbalanced.

Living in balance will be considered incredibly radical. We need to make sure we are being fed, having fellowship, and encouraging one another, but we also need to make sure their is an outflow for what God is imparting and pouring into us. Live radical. Next time you want to go do something for God, go and do it for the least, because that is where you will find Him.

Get a pen and paper. Start your own list. It is time to get balanced.

6 FRUITFULNESS

Fruitfulness

Much of the western church is facing a crisis today. We have countries where the majority of people have some belief in God. A majority even believes in the person of Jesus, and have some understanding of who He is. At the same time, however, these populations have a dwindling number of people who are interested in attending church.

It seems that even those in the church, at some point in their lives, are coming to a crossroads when they are asking, *What is the point?* Many are saying, *I know I love God, but there must be more to it than simply sitting in a seat or pew an hour a week.* There are now countless messages, books, and songs about how much we love God, but we are not too sure about the church.

In the last decades, we have especially seen the majority of the youth and young adults in traditional churches become less involved. In fact, the majority of the present generation who grew up attending church have left. Some leave because of lack of interest, some because they are bored, but a large percentage were simply never truly engaged at any point in their lives. Many claim they never saw a connection between church attendance and the message they heard.

Many of the issues that churches have struggled with, internally, are only about surface problems. These issues do not address the underlying cause of stagnation. When there are problems or when things are not moving forward, some blame the clergy or the church leadership. Some blame the music, the style, and the location. The list goes on and on. However, when Christians are aggravated, uneasy, or discontent, it may be a sign of something much deeper.

Even as the Bible begins, we see that man was given a direction and a purpose from God. *"So God created man in his own image, in the image of God he created him; male and female he created them. God blessed them and said to them, 'Be fruitful and increase in number; fill the earth and subdue it'"* (Genesis 1:27-28, NIV) Whether you want to call it instinct or our nature, every living thing finds a way to recreate or reproduce itself. This is even more true for Christians. Right in the DNA of every believer is a God-given desire to be fruitful and multiply. This is most evident when people first start their walk with Christ. It is difficult to get them to stop talking about what Jesus has done for them. They simply want everyone to know.

utine will get to even the best of us. If you are liv-
less version of Christianity, you will always have
some kind of discontentment or longing for something different. Many have tried to fix the problem of discontentment by changing programs, services, and styles... by
changing churches, or by leaving altogether. Too often, in
the end, all this has done is brought even more confusion
and fighting, and caused more people to leave churches.

It must be understood that this inner longing we all
have to be "fruitful" is God-given. It is not evil or something
to be feared. Instead, it is something to be encouraged and
let loose. Throughout the Scriptures, we are told in many
ways to spur one another on to good works. In fact, we
were created to do good works (Hebrews 10:14, Ephesians
2:10).

In Colossians 1:10, we see a picture of what spiritual
maturity looks like: *"Then the way you live will always honor
and please the Lord, and your lives will produce every kind
of good fruit. All the while, you will grow as you learn to
know God better and better"* (NLT). A Christ-like life is a
fruitful life. Discipleship is the means to release the burden
that God has put into the heart of every believer.

Presently, this is an exciting generation because it is one
that desires to participate, make a difference, and to see
Christianity lived rather than just heard. There is certainly a
longing in the hearts of this generation to see the teachings
of the Church lived out and impacting our world. It is not a
call to go to church, but rather to be the Church. Being part

of a community where you can't participate, add to, create in, or influence does not interest most of us today.

As I mentioned earlier, it has been argued that in nature the sign of maturity is the ability to reproduce. As believers mature, it could be expected that the same should also apply to them. But it goes even further. Any adult male can have offspring. However, not everyone who helps create a life has the intention, ability, or desire to raise a child into a man or woman like themselves. There is certainly much more interest in procreation than in raising children.

In John 15, we learn so much of how living a fruitful life works. In verse sixteen, it states, *"I appointed you to go and produce lasting fruit"* (NLT). We are not simply called to produce fruit, but to produce something that lasts. We have to see fruitfulness through the eyes of discipleship. Evangelism alone does not produce lasting fruit. Conversion plus discipleship does.

Something else we learn in John 15 is that we cannot produce lasting fruit, or anything for that matter, without staying connected to God. At times, we assume that to be fruitful or make disciples we will have to work more. This chapter, in fact, teaches something different. We produce fruit because of our connection to the source of life. It is not about us witnessing more, but rather growing in our knowledge and relationship with Him and letting the river of living water flow from our hearts and lives (John 7:38).

In Ezekiel 47, we are told about a river that flows from the temple. In verse nine, is says, *"Life will flourish wherever this water flows"* (NLT). It is in 1 Corinthians 6:19 that we hear, *"Don't you realize that your body is the temple of the Holy Spirit, who lives in you and was given to you by God? You do not belong to yourself"* (NLT). This life that flows from the temple now resides in us and needs to flow out. But we have to understand that the source of life and fruitfulness is not us. It is God. By staying connected to Him, we become witnesses, we become fruitful, and everywhere we go, "life will flourish."

IDEA

Buy a Dog

We need to find connecting points with other people, whether it be our immediate neighbours or those in our community. These connecting points may be the local coffee shop, a bowling league, or a softball team. The list of possibilities is endless. The real question for you is, are you ever putting yourself in places to meet new people and start friendships?

You really don't have to buy a dog. But it may not hurt. Three years ago, our family got a new puppy. He was a cute six-pound puppy. If I am ever feeling like I need to meet some new people, all I have to do is take my dog for a walk. Our small puppy, which is appropriately named Bear, now weighs about two hundred pounds and is a drooling St. Bernard. If I step out my door and walk through town, I am guaranteed to have many conversations with people on the street. Bear is one of our connecting points. At the time, we thought we were just getting a dog.

What are your connecting points?

7 | TAKING THE PRESSURE OFF

Taking the Pressure Off

When I was younger, I have to admit I wanted to save the world. In fact, I thought this was my true and high calling in life. I put pressure on myself to do a great deal. So much of this was borne out of a sincere desire to spread hope and the Gospel to those who had never heard it, and would be lost without it.

We need to thank God that in our youth we have great zeal, because the world would never change without it. Throughout history, it has been youth and young adults who have sparked and caused the rise and downfall of so many movements. However, having a bit of wisdom mixed with zeal is what makes us truly effective.

In looking at the life of Jesus, I have wondered, as many others likely have, why did He do what He did? Or perhaps the better question is, why did God choose to do it that

way? Why did Jesus limit himself to sharing with only so
many people? Why, if God wanted to save the world,
would Jesus only have had such a small number of disciples?
Why would He only have travelled in such a limited area?
Why didn't He heal everyone on earth, instead of just those
brought to him personally?

If we had the opportunity to do it our way, we would
certainly do it differently. We definitely would not have
chosen to send Jesus two thousand years ago. It would make
more sense to have Him here now. Then we could set up
huge crusades, television events, webcasts, podcasts, bring
in bands, set up sound and lighting systems, and have huge
ministries. We would have Jesus TV. We could buy Him His
own personal jet to get Him from event to event without
delays. We certainly would get Him on the talk show circuit,
and even, likely, on Oprah. Instead, in every way, Jesus
opted for something different and much simpler. But why?

I now believe the answer is that He was setting the
foundation for a movement that would bring long-term and
worldwide transformation. He was demonstrating how the
Kingdom would spread and setting something in place that
would outlast His time on earth. He was modeling how to
produce and create lasting fruit in every generation until
His return.

Whether we are comfortable with it or not, His way is
the right way. That is not to diminish any of those other
evangelistic tools—God certainly has and will continue to
use all of those things in the future. However, without fol-

lowing the model that Jesus lived, none of those tools will produce unlimited, lasting fruit.

I have found that there are two reactions people have when presented with this view of discipleship. For some, there is huge excitement when they realize what they have been missing in their lives. Certainly, living like Jesus seems like a good idea.

However, some people are fearful. You may be thinking, *Wow, this is all great, but where on earth am I going to find the time? This is way too big and too much responsibility for me.* When presented with the task of making disciples and sharing the Gospel with the world, the enormity of the task simply scares people. Add to this the teaching that you are to disciple all those people and we know we are going to fail, because we are not able to do it all. We have put a burden and responsibility on many people that is simply overwhelming.

It is true that the will of the Father is that none would perish, and I know that Jesus came to seek and save the lost (Matthew 18:14, Luke 19:10). We certainly need to gain the same compassion for the lost and hurting as Jesus had and tried to pass on to his followers. I also believe that there is a heaven and hell. I know that God has created us as eternal beings that will, in fact, spend an eternity somewhere.

When I come to grips with these things, I want to do something. I even want to do something drastic to make the biggest difference I can in the life of as many people as possible. One of the things I have never understood about most churches is that, if we really believe people are lost, then how in good conscience can we just keep on holding services for ourselves and never get out of our buildings to truly impact our communities?

Before going any further, you should hear something. Jesus said, *"My yoke is easy and my burden is light"* (Matthew 11:30, NIV). The task given to us was not to be an impossible or depressing burden. Instead it is to be an incredible journey that will take us through great victories, and even some great sorrows.

These seem to be two extremes. A majority of churches and ministries seem to find themselves on one side or the other, either very evangelistic or using a very laidback approach. One would assume there is a balance somewhere in the middle that works.

I do not mean to sound heretical, but I believe neither solution, even in balance, is the answer. I now believe I was never meant to save the world, and neither are you. Maybe we need to stop our own striving, or lack thereof, and simply learn from what Jesus did. To follow Jesus' model, I may, in fact, preach and speak to the masses in my lifetime. I may pastor hundreds and thousands of people, but, like Jesus, I need to remember to disciple the few.

In looking at the gospels, we see that Jesus had many circles of influence. He had the masses to which He taught and shared the truths about the Kingdom. Then there were the hundreds or thousands of people who followed and took in much of his teaching. There were the seventy-two

who He sent out to tell the Good News. Closer still were
twelve men, who Jesus had a unique relationship with, and
they went with Him almost everywhere. Then, out of that
twelve, He had His three. And, out of those three, there was
the one who laid his head on His breast.

The reason most people are scared of Jesus' way of discipleship is that they know they cannot disciple all the ones
they are leading or feel they need to reach. The truth is that
you need to stop trying, and realize that if Jesus, in His wisdom, didn't do it, then neither should you. Perhaps it is
even wrong, prideful, and arrogant to think we can or
should do what Jesus never did.

What if we took the pressure off? What if all we ask of
people is that, in their lifetime, they need to make a few
disciples, not save the world? Some may look at this and
think that this is a lesser plan; however, it is not.

By investing in the few, I will produce much more lasting
fruit than if I keep to my own methods. Our manmade
methods are all based on the principles of addition. Jesus'
model was based on multiplication. When we realize that if
each one of us makes disciples wherever it is God sends us,
we affect towns, cities, and countries for generations to
come.

Discipleship is not about the numbers. It is about doing
what works. It is not about being busy. I believe the Scriptures challenge us to help people become mature, to have
depth of character, and to become radical change agents
on this planet. If you can help two, four, or even twelve

people accomplish that in your lifetime, it is going to be far more effective than producing fifty apathetic, pew sitting, content, powerless, and absolutely fruitless church attendees. By doing less, and being more focused, you can in fact accomplish much more.

There is a cost to being a disciple, which includes dying to our own ways, methods, and striving. Discipleship is about investing in a bigger future. It is about truly sowing into the harvest. Psalm 126:5-6 says, *"Those who plant in tears will harvest with shouts of joy. They weep as they go to plant their seed, but they sing as they return with the harvest"* (NLT). There is a joy that comes when we see results for our sowing, planting, and investing. Even though the process may in fact cost us something—even some tears and some work—the payoff is worth it. If we do what Jesus did, we will surely see a harvest.

IDEA

Being Yourself

When I think of the pressure people put on themselves, it is no wonder they are stressed out. Perhaps even thoughts of discipleship have been stressing you out. I know that the fears of how to meet and connect with other people can be overwhelming. Let's pick an easy starting point, though. You. This should be something you are familiar with.

Consider for a moment that you are who you are because God made you that way. You have unique interests, skills, and thoughts. God created you with such diversity. While some churches try to make its whole congregation into one type of cookie-cutter person, this is totally wrong. If God wanted us that way, that is how He would have made us.

When we are all the same, we only reach into one circle of influence in a community. This is why some churches only seem to reach one type of person, or one segment of a community. However, what if we encouraged people to just be themselves and impact their own circle of influence, friends, and environment? With diversity, our influence is greater.

It is okay to be who God made you to be. I have a few interests in my life that, in a sense, welcome me into certain "tribes" of people. When I am driving my motorcycle, I can simply walk into a setting where all the bikers are and be part of the group. That is because it is who I am. Someone else could walk into that setting and be totally uncomfortable and feel out of place, because that is not who they are. In a sense, we force people into places they don't fit, and this causes them to become frustrated.

Think about what God has put in your life. Think about what gifts you have, what interests you have. You do not have to be like everyone else. This journey may start for you when you begin to let God use *you*. That doesn't mean you rush out and just do things for Him. Let Him use who the person He has created you to be. Just be yourself. Perhaps God has made you to be who you are because that is exactly who He needs right now, right where you are, to reach those around you.

8 NO MORE BIG LIGHTS

No More Big Lights

There is a powerful song we sang at my last church called "To the Ends of the Earth," by Hillsong in Australia. In the song, the people declare, "I will go to the ends of the earth, for You." It is a wonderful call to join the mission to which God has called us. If you have never heard the song, take some time to experience it and get to the heart of it.

What do you think would happen to a church if suddenly everyone said, "Okay, I will to go. I want to be involved"? After the shocked leaders composed themselves, most of them would actually have a hard time even comprehending where to begin. If we had a group of people who all wanted to participate in ministry, the truth is we wouldn't even know what to do with them.

Most of us have only seen church models where a limited number of leaders led larger groups of spectators. If we are honest, we will realize that is impossible to involve everyone in most modern church structures in roles other than spectators. But though it is true that in large groups it is impossible to involve everyone, is this all that we were meant to have? Even in the life of Jesus, we see how He taught to the masses. But afterward He would sit down and explain and discuss things with His disciples.

This is one of the reasons why people are bored or disillusioned with church attendance. We are not even sure what to do with everyone who comes. They are unengaged because we have never given them anything really meaningful to do. In fact, we have given them a very skewed idea of ministry. For the most part, the only ministry they have ever seen modeled is a teaching ministry (preaching), some music ministry (special songs, choirs, worship teams) or, perhaps some more creative models (drama, dance, reading, etc).

One of the biggest reasons people who attend a spectator-based church never become mature is that they have never had an outlet to live out what they have heard. They may be able to live out parts of Christ likeness, like His character, but not His deeds. Part of learning is practical, and can't just be taught verbally. We challenge people to live something out in their everyday lives which they have never actually seen modeled for them.

In a sense, we have made our community think that people who have a teaching gift are the embodiment of what a successful Christian should look like. On most Sundays, it is a few individuals who do most of the "ministry."

However, what about those who aren't gifted in that manner? What if they can't sing, or even perhaps really shouldn't? The truth is that the vast majority of people are not gifted speakers or singers, but these are the only gifts most churches publicly present. We even go to the extreme in saying that these few people have a higher calling than those watching. This is just another way we make people think, *We better let them do everything because it seems that is who God chose to do it.*

People have a skewed view of what ministry is because of what they have seen. This does not mean, however, that we shouldn't recognize the talents and abilities of these gifted people, because they are extremely needed. What is lacking is a proper understanding that they are only presenting one gifting of ministry, of which there are many types. For example, in Ephesians 4:11 we read, *"Now these are the gifts Christ gave to the church: the apostles, the prophets, the evangelists, and the pastors and teachers"* (NLT).

It seems Scripture would teach that all these different types of gifts are needed to bring maturity to the Church. In 1 Corinthians 12:18-22, it states, *"But our bodies have many parts, and God has put each part just where he wants it. How strange a body would be if it had only one part! Yes, there are many parts, but only one body. The eye can never say to the hand, 'I don't need you.' The head can't say to the feet, 'I don't need you.' In fact, some parts of the body that seem weakest and least important are actually the most necessary"* (NLT). Scripture even teaches how much we really need what may seem the least important.

While there are many different types of gifts and ministries we can operate in that can seem quite spectacular, there are some we can miss. For example, perhaps some things that are really necessary are not done publicly, such as prayer and discipleship. Maybe we have left all the ministry to those who seem to have these so-called "important gifts," and have therefore lost our fruitfulness. We need the whole body to operate together, not just a part.

Not only can we gain a skewed or limited perspective of what ministry is, I believe we also have a wrong view of what success is. Mark 8:36 says, *"And what do you benefit if you gain the whole world but lose your own soul?"* (NLT) Fame or importance in the Church is not success in the Kingdom of God. That would be contrary to Christ's life and teachings.

I look up to many people. I have seen or heard of some great examples of Christian living and people who have done noble things. When it comes to success, though, I can think of two examples of what I now consider success in the Kingdom of God.

Several years ago, as I was working with a team at a YWAM base in Monterrey, Mexico, some of the staff told us about a woman we needed to meet. They drove me and a few of my team to her modest house in a neighbourhood where most of us would never consider living. When we got there, I was welcomed to a very full house. This woman, who

ɔt known outside of her own neighbourhood, had
ᴗ. fifty orphan children living in her house. She had
changed her entire life to help children who had no one to
take care of them.

When I think of this older lady, I know that many people wouldn't think of her as successful. She is not wealthy,
not well known, has given up her own space for others, does
not have a well known ministry, and has no great status.
However, if the greatest in the Kingdom of God is the one
who serves, or if there really is no greater love than to lay
down your life for your friends, than this woman is a picture
of success in the eyes of God. Success in the Kingdom of
God does not mean we have to be the center of attention.
Rather, it is okay if those we are serving are.

I am amazed at how much of our outreach involves us
being in front of people. We sing, put on productions,
plays, and dramas, and go on TV. Perhaps God is looking
for people who will put someone else on display. If what we
do for the least is really being done to and for Him, than
shouldn't He be at the center?

In Ecclesiastes 4:7-8, we learn such an important truth. *"I
observed yet another example of something meaningless
under the sun. This is the case of a man who is all alone,
without a child or a brother, yet who works hard to gain as
much wealth as he can. But then he asks himself, 'Who am I
working for? Why am I giving up so much pleasure now?' It
is all so meaningless and depressing"* (NLT). We can spend
our lives on ourselves, or on our church, and give nothing

away to anyone else. Who cares? It is all meaningless… But it goes even further. When we have nobody willing to give away what God has given them, our whole Christian walk becomes depressing.

When Jesus looked at the crowds with compassion, what did He say to pray for? Did He say, "Father send more pastors? Ministers? Superstars? Bands?" No. He said, "Send labourers." Today, we need the Church to operate in its giftings, where everyone is asked to labour. Discipleship is one of those ministries that is for everyone in some way. It is how we labour for the Kingdom. It is time to step out of the crowds and begin to be the answer to the prayer for labourers and say, "I will go to the ends of the earth for You."

9 | REBORN

Reborn

As I have shared about discipleship over the past few years, I have seen and heard a pretty mixed reaction. Many questions arise, because when we are challenged with something new our first thought is, *How will I add this to what I am already doing?* We live in a busy culture, and hardly anyone can add something as big as discipling others into their already complicated life.

That may not be the correct starting point, though. Maybe we need to look at this in a new perspective and even question, *Should I be doing everything I am doing now?* You were not meant to burn out or to have no time left over for your personal life and family. While we know we are called to be fruitful in our lives, discipleship is not meant to be something we force people into. It has to be a work of God in our lives. Perhaps we need to re-evaluate where we are putting our efforts instead of just adding more things into our lives.

> *"And no one puts new wine into old wineskins. For the old skins would burst from the pressure, spilling the wine and ruining the skins. New wine is stored in new wineskins so that both are preserved."*
>
> (Matthew 9:17, NLT)

Many years ago, I heard Pastor César Castellanos, who leads a cell church (a collection of small groups) of hundreds of thousands of people, speaking at a pastor's conference in Bogota, Columbia. He was telling everyone that they needed to be reborn into the vision of multiplication, much like when we are born again spiritually. I remember hearing this and thinking that it sounded like a difficult or strange teaching.

Now, after trying to live this out, I have to say that I now believe I understand some of what he meant. Jesus' discipleship model is not something that can be added to an existing program-based model. In fact, trying to add it onto an already busy schedule can be quite destructive. Just as it says in Matthew 9:17, a new wine can burst or destroy an old wineskin. Many churches and ministries who have tried to add this type of ministry to their existing model have completely failed, or faced various levels of self-inflicted turmoil. It is incredibly difficult, or even impossible, to pour new wine into an old wineskin. Without a death and rebirth, it can never happen.

Many individuals, churches, or denominations want to turn back the hands of time so that they can reinvent themselves or return to their fruitful days. Many groups have decided they want live in the 1970s, or in the 1800s, 1400s, or various other time periods. However, instead of picking a later time period, why not go right back to the original instead of someone's else's interpretation or version?

This is not a journey that many may even want to take. It could be costly. As we know, Jesus instructed us to count the cost. In the following section, we are going to look at how Jesus' model works contrary to how we may want do things. Again, I would ask you to pray that God would challenge you to become more like His Son, Jesus. If there are things within us that need to die, I pray that we will let them go so that we can walk, and even run, in freedom.

SECTION
TWO

10 JESUS THE SON

Jesus the Son

There are certainly endless lessons we can learn from the scriptures. There are guidelines, encouragement, directions, and life-giving words. There are things that we are instructed to do and some things we are instructed to do without. However, throughout the scriptures, there are certain statements that just seem to really stand out. Things we just cannot do without. When we are talking about discipleship, this may be the one lesson we cannot forget. Without a proper understanding of discipleship, we may miss everything. In fact, there is a very strong directive here. It says, "You must."

> *You must have the same attitude that Christ*
> *Jesus had.*
> *Though he was God, he did not think of*
> *equality with God as something to cling to.*

Instead, he gave up his divine privileges; he
took the humble position of a slave and
was born as a human being.
When he appeared in human form, he
humbled himself in obedience to God and
died a criminal's death on a cross.
Therefore, God elevated him to the place of
highest honor and gave him the name
above all other names, that at the name of
Jesus every knee should bow, in heaven and on
earth and under the earth, and every
tongue confess that Jesus Christ is Lord, to
the glory of God the Father.

(Philippians 2:5-11, NLT)

A few years ago, I was sitting with a young man who was planning on attending seminary. We were listening to a powerful sermon from a seasoned minister. He shared from several scriptures and told many amazing stories about how God had worked in his life.

In our discussion afterwards, this young man expressed his desire to be a great speaker like this gentleman we had just heard. While of course this was a noble idea, I gave a word of caution. I shared that this man had a story to tell because his message came out of his experience. He had a wealth of wisdom to share because God had formed him through the stories he told. I told this young man that he needed to go live his life for God so that one day he would have a message worth sharing.

Too often, we are guilty of wanting to sidestep life's process and take steps to build our own kingdoms and move into greatness. We want the results without ever paying the price. We want the glory without the pain of the cross.

Yet it almost seems that Jesus had no plans of greatness for Himself. In fact, everything He did worked to the contrary. I am sure that even His disciples wondered, *When are You going to rise up and free us from Rome?* Yet even in the humility of His birth, who His parents were, and the animal He rode into Jerusalem, there was no running after self-glorification. Jesus seemed content with just letting the Father lift him up.

To truly model the character of Jesus, we have to understand humility and "sonship." According to the scripture in Philippians, "we must" take on this attitude. In fact, it is through humility that He can teach us how to live this out. *"He leads the humble in doing right, teaching them his way"* (Psalm 25:9, NLT)

We may have thoughts of what it means to be a leader, but Jesus broke almost all definitions. In Matthew 18:4, Jesus shares his thoughts on greatness when He says, *"So anyone who becomes as humble as this little child is the greatest in the Kingdom of Heaven"* (NLT).

In Matthew 23:12, He even warned us that danger was ahead if we tried to become great ourselves. *"But those who exalt themselves will be humbled, and those who humble themselves will be exalted"* (NLT). He even instructs us that any "lifting" that needs to be done, needs to come from God. *"Humble yourselves before the Lord, and he will lift you up in honor"* (James 4:10, NLT).

Though He Himself was God, Jesus seemed content to operate as a son. It was only in the Father's love that He operated. It seems so true that, while many people, ministers, and leaders want position, unless we take on sonship, we risk moving up without God lifting us. This is where Jesus' leadership differs from any others. We become great by becoming less.

If you want to be a great father to others, first you must learn what it means to be a good son. If you are striving to disciple others, you must put yourself in a position to be discipled. If you want God to use you in greater things, you must do your best with what you have now. *"The master was full of praise. 'Well done, my good and faithful servant. You have been faithful in handling this small amount, so now I will give you many more responsibilities. Let's celebrate together!'"* (Matthew 25:21, NLT) The message is always the same: more comes from the master. We do not have to strive for greatness. We must strive for sonship.

Without sonship, we operate from a dangerous place. As people who are serving and discipling others, we can try to lead people into something we have never operated in ourselves. We can even be doing something worse, in that we are asking people to do something we are unwilling to do ourselves. If we cannot submit and become sons, we cannot be kingdom leaders—unless the kingdom is our own.

Throughout the Bible, we see that blessing flows from father to son. Unless we put ourselves in that place, we can never receive the blessing and impartation that happens through this relationship. Blessing flowed from Abraham to Isaac, from Isaac to Jacob, from Paul to Timothy, from Elijah to Elisha, and from the Father to Jesus. This is often a painful switch. For too many so-called Christian leaders, the words, *"Yet I want your will to be done, not mine,"* have never crossed their lips (Luke 22:42, NLT).

What is part of the beauty of Jesus is that He is the Truth and He is the Word. Perfect integrity. Life, deed, actions, thoughts, and words all working together. In Mark 9:35, He gave the disciples these instructions, *"Whoever wants to be first must take last place and be the servant of everyone else"* (NLT). Then we see how Jesus was even willing to lay down His life for each one of us, and to serve the Father.

Throughout Scripture, we see how others took on this example that Jesus gave us. In 2 Corinthians 4:5, we see a picture from Paul's life. *"You see, we don't go around preaching about ourselves. We preach that Jesus Christ is Lord, and we ourselves are your servants for Jesus' sake"* (NLT). Great leaders lay down their lives to serve, and do not look to be served. It is the great paradox of the upside-down kingdom. The last will be first. The servant is the greatest. The humble are lifted up. The Son is the King.

IDEA

Look in a Mirror

In case you think you may be the only Christian who doesn't read their Bible consistently, you are not. Most Christians only read their Bible once a week, and that is while they are in church.

In James 1:23-24, we read, *"For if you listen to the word and don't obey, it is like glancing at your face in a mirror. You see yourself, walk away, and forget what you look like"* (NLT). We are told we not only need to read or hear the Word, but we are to do what it says.

Here is some incentive for you to read your Bible more. If you have ever looked a mirror, you may or may not have been happy with what you saw, and simply sitting and staring into a mirror does not change your appearance. However, while sitting in front of a mirror, people use that opportunity to apply make-up, fix their hair, shave, and do numerous other things to make themselves look better.

The Bible is different, though. It is the one mirror that you can stare into that causes your appearance to change. The more you look into it, the better looking you get. It causes a change in your countenance, your attitude, your thoughts, and your demeanour. It not only changes your looks, but also your walk. You begin to look up and forward instead of down. It even lights up the path you are journey-ing on.

The longer and more intense you look into this mirror, the more you will look and act like Jesus. Get into the Word.

11 JESUS' UPSIDE DOWN KINGDOM

Jesus' Upside Down Kingdom

There are several instances in the gospels where the disciples argue amongst themselves about which of them is be the greatest. The fact that they argued over this is not surprising. It seems to be part of human nature. What is really surprising, though, is when these arguments broke out.

One such argument happens after the Transfiguration takes place. Here, Jesus is revealed in His glory in front of several disciples. It is shortly after that when they begin to discuss which of them is the greatest. In Mark 9:33-34, it states, *"After they arrived at Capernaum and settled in a house, Jesus asked his disciples, 'What were you discussing out on the road?' But they didn't answer, because they had been arguing about which of them was the greatest"* (NLT).

It was in these times that Jesus challenged them to re-think the way they thought His Kingdom really worked. In verse 35, it says, *"He sat down, called the twelve disciples over to him, and said, 'Whoever wants to be first must take last place and be the servant of everyone else'"* (NLT). He began to call them into a new way of thinking. He was telling them to change. He was calling them out of the natural king-dom, and into His, which functions in a radically different way.

Another instance when the disciples argued about who was greatest was at the last supper. It was here that Jesus talked about laying His life down and what real love was. The disciples' argument seems so out of place in this setting. Yet perhaps it is there to show that this will be one of our biggest struggles.

In Luke 22:24-27, we start to get a picture of the con-trast between the Kingdom Jesus was proclaiming and the kingdoms of this world. *"Then they began to argue among themselves about who would be the greatest among them. Jesus told them, 'In this world the kings and great men lord it over their people, yet they are called "friends of the peo-ple." But among you it will be different. Those who are the greatest among you should take the lowest rank, and the leader should be like a servant. Who is more important, the one who sits at the table or the one who serves? The one who sits at the table, of course. But not here! For I am among you as one who serves'"* (NLT).

Jesus strikes at the concept of lording power over others and calls them to embrace something new. He says, "Among you it will be different." He is calling them, and us, to walk in a different kingdom, where success is not about being in charge, being the master, or having power. In His kingdom, a leader must serve. In most places, a leader takes the place of honour, but Jesus is clear, "Not here." In His upside-down kingdom, even the King who was among them served.

Jesus seems to leave no doubt as to what kind of leadership He did and did not want. In John 13, we see one of the most intriguing stories that takes place in the Bible. Again, it is one of the conversations that occurs during the last supper between Jesus and His disciples before His crucifixion.

> It was just before the Passover Feast. Jesus knew that the time had come for him to leave this world and go to the Father. Having loved his own who were in the world, he now showed them the full extent of his love.
>
> The evening meal was being served, and the devil had already prompted Judas Iscariot, son of Simon, to betray Jesus. Jesus knew that the Father had put all things under his power, and that he had come from God and was returning to God; so he got up from the meal, took off his outer clothing, and wrapped a

towel around his waist. After that, he poured water into a basin and began to wash his disciples' feet, drying them with the towel that was wrapped around him.

He came to Simon Peter, who said to him, "Lord, are you going to wash my feet?"

Jesus replied, "You do not realize now what I am doing, but "later you will understand."

"No," said Peter, "you shall never wash my feet."

Jesus answered, "Unless I wash you, you have no part with me."

"Then, Lord," Simon Peter replied, "not just my feet but my hands and my head as well!" (…)

When he had finished washing their feet, he put on his clothes and returned to his place. "Do you understand what I have done for you?" he asked them. "You call me 'Teacher' and 'Lord,' and rightly so, for that is what I am. Now that I, your Lord and Teacher, have washed your feet, you also should wash one another's feet. I have set you an example that you should do as I have done for you. I tell you the truth, no servant is greater than his master, nor is a messenger greater than the one who

> *sent him. Now that you know these things, you*
> *will be blessed if you do them.*
>
> (John 13:1-9,12-17, NIV)

It should be noted that this happens within the same timeframe that Jesus mentions that one of them will betray Him, and also that Peter will also deny Him. In that setting, Jesus washes His disciples' feet. These were the feet of doubters, deniers, betrayers, and the questioning. This is also the time when Jesus gives one of the strongest rebukes.

Even when Jesus was telling Peter that he would deny Him, Jesus never said what He did in this situation. When Jesus gets to Peter, Peter says, "No, you shall never wash my feet." The response Jesus gives him is, "Unless I wash you, you have no part with me." Peter, when challenged, gives one of the best responses anyone could ever give: "Then, Lord, not just my feet but my hands and my head as well!" And with that, he jumped into this kingdom with his whole being.

Peter was not trying to be disrespectful when he first refused Jesus. His whole life had taught him that this job was not for a teacher, rabbi, or leader. Peter likely thought that if someone was going to be washing feet, then he should be washing Jesus' feet. Yet Jesus' strong message to him was, "Among you it will be different." In fact, if Peter didn't let Him do this, he couldn't have any part of Him.

For Peter, and us today, we are left with a message. Just as Jesus, who is the Lord, washed their feet, we must to the same for each other. In this upside-down kingdom, disciple-ship means serving. It is where the one who leads give the places of honour to those around him. If we refuse to live in this different kind of kingdom, it means we are still walking in our own.

12 JESUS THE FRIEND

Jesus the Friend

We often have a hard time interpreting Scripture because the first thing we want to do is apply it to our setting, our way of thinking, our life, our church, and our ministries. But there are many things that Jesus did with His disciples that just don't seem to fit with our lives, culture, or setting. The easiest thing to do when we run across these scriptures is simply avoid talking about them. However, our cultures aren't based on the same principles as Jesus' Kingdom.

I fully believe that God has called people to certain tasks in life. I believe that all of us are called to disciple others in whatever setting or arena we are find ourselves. I also believe that God calls people into bivocational, and some to full-time, ministry. Some are called to be teachers, pastors, apostles, prophets, and evangelists. No matter what your part in this whole body of believers, each part is only a part.

While not disrespecting these callings and gifts, I have found that some have developed an "us and them" mentality. There is the clergy, the laymen, the boards, the deacons, and so on. In a way, many churches and denominations create a kind of caste system that traps people into levels of importance. While we may all be called, some appear to have a higher calling.

In looking at the life of Jesus, and what He did for the disciples, there seems to be a shift away from this hierarchal approach. The first are not first in His kingdom. However, the differences extend beyond how we are to treat one another.

It is entirely possible for you to serve another person without really caring for them as an individual. You can serve another person without having to be a friend or really getting involved. For example, we can look at the poor as just a group of people, and skip over the individuals. We can go and hand out sandwiches and gifts at Christmas, only to then quickly return to the safety of our church buildings. It is possible to do all of these right things with less than perfect motives.

You may even be able to serve the less fortunate because you understand that whatever you do for them, you are doing for Christ. Discipleship goes beyond that. It doesn't cause you to go to the "poor" or some other group of a generic description. It causes you to go help Susan, Matthew, or Jacob, knowing the names of those you meet.

In a sense, we have separated ministry and friendship. It is impossible to truly disciple someone you are not friends with. We have levels of leadership that we feel we need to protect, because our ministry models require it. However, that does not mean all manmade models are Biblical.

In Hosea 2:16, the prophet spoke about a change that was coming. *"'When that day comes,' says the Lord, 'you will call me "my husband" instead of "my master"'"* (NLT). There seems to be a difference coming in how we view our relationship with God. There is a shift from seeing God as an all-powerful impersonal being in the sky to a partner we can know intimately.

At the last supper, Jesus says to His disciples, *"I no longer call you servants, because a servant does not know his master's business. Instead, I have called you friends, for everything that I learned from my Father I have made known to you"* (John 15:15, NIV). Jesus Himself looked at these men and calls them "friends." Some may argue that this is stated only because He was going to die to make peace between God and men, but I believe there is more to it than that.

It is said in the context of Jesus asking a group of disciples to follow Him. It is with the group of people that Jesus had spent several years with on a daily basis. It is within the context of the group who ministered together, laughed together, and had meals together. We cannot forget that, while Jesus was God, He was also human. He was a man in need of fellowship, friendship, and time with others.

In many circles, it is believed that we cannot be friends with those we lead or serve. Part of this belief stems from the reality that ministers cannot be good friends with everyone in a church. However, we have already established that neither can they disciple a whole church. There does need to be a connection with those who are being discipled by every leader. To do otherwise would be trying to disciple in a way other than how Jesus did it.

Part of discipleship is relationship. This is scary, because we are not perfect like Jesus. It is also far more comfortable to lead out of our strengths than our weaknesses, which people who are close to us will see. It is difficult for a boss to be friends with all of his employees. Too often, we think that this kind of relationship translates into our Christian walk. However, in a modern-day work setting, the employees serve the boss. In the Kingdom of God, the employees are served.

When we become friends with people, we take ourselves off the pedestal and become a common labourer. When we become friends, we cannot lead by power. We have to lead by example. It would be wonderful for each believer to have a relationship with Jesus, like the relationship mentioned in Proverbs 18:24: *"A man of many companions may come to ruin, but there is a friend who sticks closer than a brother"* (NIV).

There is incredible power in the bonds of friendship. Ecclesiastes 4:9-12 sums it up best. *"Two people are better off than one, for they can help each other succeed. If one*

*person falls, the other can reach out and help. But someone
who falls alone is in real trouble. Likewise, two people lying
close together can keep each other warm. But how can one
be warm alone? A person standing alone can be attacked
and defeated, but two can stand back-to-back and conquer.
Three are even better, for a triple-braided cord is not easily
broken"* (NLT). One of the strengths of discipleship is the
bonds of real friendship of those involved. There, also, is
great protection. This is seen when Jesus would only send
out His disciples in pairs.

We do not always think of hospitality as a gift, but it
does come from God. Consider these verses:

> *"When God's people are in need, be ready to
> help them. Always be eager to practice hospi-
> tality."*
>
> (Romans 12:13, NLT)

> *"Offer hospitality to one another without
> grumbling."*
>
> (1 Peter 4:9-10, NIV)

> *"Be devoted to one another in brotherly love.
> Honor one another above yourselves... Share
> with God's people who are in need. Practice
> hospitality."*
>
> (Romans 12:10,13, NIV)

When it comes to our relationships with one another, we need to be open to receive and give love. We also need to invite friends into our lives.

What is evident in Jesus' friendship offer to the disciples is that it was not based on circumstance. Despite the fact that Peter was going to deny Him, this friendship was still offered. It was not based on whether or not they were perfect, or even close to it.

Over the years, I have had the unfortunate opportunity to witness how badly many former leaders have been treated after they fell or left ministry. It almost seemed as if all the so-called ministry friends they had were only friends as long as they were doing well or were equals. That kind of friendship is not "closer than a brother," is it? Family does not leave when everything goes wrong. Brothers don't abandon one another when they fall. It is family who can pick a brother up and restore him, gently, with wisdom and love.

When I think of some of these situations that I have seen and dealt with, I realize how shallow so many relationships between believers can be. We have to ask ourselves, are we only befriending someone because they are our Christian project, or do we welcome them into our lives? If there is a prayer we as the church need to pray, it is that God would teach us how to be friends. We need to pray that we would learn to truly bear one another's burdens, encourage one another, pray for one another, and most

importantly love one another, because this is a sign of truly
being His disciple.

> *"There is no greater love than to lay down
> one's life for one's friends."*
>
> John 15:13 (NLT)

IDEA

Don't Go Alone

There are many verses in the Bible that talk about the strength that comes from numbers. Even when Jesus sent the disciples out, He sent them in pairs and never alone. There is protection, encouragement, mentoring, and accountability when we are together.

As mentioned, people's first reaction to discipleship is often, *Where will I find the time?* Well, here is something to try. Do nothing that you don't do now. That may seem like really odd advice, at first. Instead of doing your current ministry alone, just bring someone with you. So just do what you do now, but not alone.

These doesn't just have to be ministry-type things. In fact, some of the best ministry times I've had have been over coffee, a soda, or dinner. They've come just spending time with people in many different settings. If you have interests ranging from knitting, watching movies, playing UNO—or right to extremes like skydiving—don't do these things alone all the time. Perhaps God has given you some of the interests and abilities you have as open doors into the lives of future friends.

Sometimes we try to complicate things too much. Be yourself, and use what God has given you.

13 JESUS THE FOLLOWER

Jesus the Follower

When we think of leading, we think of being up in front. Others can see and emulate what you do and who you are. As a leader, you cannot ever take people where you are not going, or have gone yourself. This means we have to be going somewhere. Jesus gives us many lessons on what leading looks like in this up-side-down kingdom, but this lesson could be the hardest to grasp. In order to lead in His way, you can never go first.

Jesus is, in fact, our leader. He is our King, Saviour, and Lord. He is also a follower. What He accomplished during His time on earth was based on his ability to follow, and not His ability to lead. At least, not by our definition of leading. Just as the greatest is the one who is the servant of all, the greatest leaders in the Kingdom are the ones who follow the best.

In the Book of John, Jesus says some incredible things about himself.

"So Jesus explained, 'I tell you the truth, the Son can do nothing by himself. He does only what he sees the Father doing. Whatever the Father does, the Son also does'" (John 5:19, NLT). There is nothing Jesus can or will do on His own. He is only set on doing what He sees the Father do first—just like we are told in John 15, that if we do not stay connected to the vine, we cannot accomplish anything. Jesus makes this same statement about Himself.

In verse 20, we get a picture of how this works. *"For the Father loves the Son and shows him everything he is doing. In fact, the Father will show him how to do even greater works than healing this man. Then you will truly be astonished"* (John 5:20, NLT). Through the loving relationship that existed between them, Jesus was able to see what the Father was doing, and then do those things Himself.

This process went beyond His actions to all that He said. *"I don't speak on my own authority. The Father who sent me has commanded me what to say and how to say it. And I know his commands lead to eternal life; so I say whatever the Father tells me to say"* (John 12:49-50, NLT). There was a message He had to share because He was being obedient to the Father.

It is through the life of Jesus that we see what it really means to follow God. We see what it means to walk in obedience. We see what is possible when a life is fully surrendered to the will of God. We get to hear what God's heart for mankind is through Jesus' words.

You can look at the life of Jesus and want to emulate His good deeds and His concern for others . Or perhaps you can just try to be a good person. However, when we think of what it means to be a disciple, it can be a mistake to think we are just to copy what Jesus did, or to get others to simply copy us. We can try to do all these good things without ever discovering the real source that makes the life of Jesus grow within us.

If we want to truly follow Jesus, like Jesus followed the Father, we have to do more than copy what He did. We need to hear what He is saying, see what He is doing, and then we need to do it. We can sometimes jump ahead, going straight to the action without really *hearing* first. Our human instinct is to want a set pattern instead of putting ourselves in a place where what we do comes out of a loving relationship with Jesus.

If we want to have something worth giving away to others, we must first hear what Jesus is saying, and then say it. This is the sign that we are truly following Christ, when we hear His voice and obey. If we want to disciple people in the ways of Christ, then we must be able to teach others how to follow Jesus in the same way Jesus followed the Father.

In John 10, Jesus tells a story that talks about how those who follow Him will hear Him. *"But the one who enters through the gate is the shepherd of the sheep. The gate-*

keeper opens the gate for him, and the sheep recognize his voice and come to him. He calls his own sheep by name and leads them out" (John 10:2-3, NLT). If we are following Jesus, we need to know and recognize His voice. This is how we know where He is going, so that we can follow.

He continues, *"After he has gathered his own flock, he walks ahead of them, and they follow him because they know his voice. They won't follow a stranger; they will run from him because they don't know his voice"* (John 10:4-5, NLT). Again, following only happens when we know the Shepherd's voice. Without His direction, we run the risk of going our own way, and leading people to other places than where Jesus is.

If it is our goal to lead, to disciple, than we to must learn what it means to follow. We cannot desire, or copy, the outcomes of a relationship with Jesus. We have to live it. You could possibly copy many of the good things Jesus did without following His voice. However, when we are listening to His voice, the things we do are going be at the right time, at the right place, and for the right people.

The people we lead also deserve a fresh word and direction. This means you have a responsibility to seek after the voice and direction of God. What is God putting on your heart to do today? These are the things you need to share with those you lead. Then, they need to see you do them. When you learn to follow His voice, you become a great leader.

IDEA

Impartation

For the past twelve years of my life, I have been involved with taking teams of people around the world on mission trips, doing humanitarian work. One of the highlights for me is getting to spend time with the people who are working in these areas. There is something contagious you can catch from people who are living out what most people only talk about doing. I want to catch what they have.

I do have some things that I hope to accomplish in my lifetime, as I am sure you do, too. When I think of some of these goals, I have to take a moment to think, *How am I ever going to see that happen in my life?* For example, if you have decided that you are going to be a doctor, you need to go out and learn medicine. You will have to study from those who have experience. You will have to watch and spend time with doctors.

If in my life I want to learn how to be a soul winner, or someone who disciples others, then there is something I have to do: I need to seek out people who are gifted and are being used by God in these areas. They have been imparted with these gifts for a few reasons. First, it is to be effective where they are. Secondly, it is to impart it to others.

Find people full of passion for God and those who don't know Him. Spend time with them. Learn from them. Walk with them. Catch what they have.

SECTION
THREE

14 A CALL TO FATHERHOOD

A Call to Fatherhood

There are many definitions of a father or mother. All of them agree that it is much more than simply having the ability to produce offspring. Being a parent includes both producing and raising children. It speaks of protecting and providing for them as they grow. It speaks of imparting life's lessons, and passing on the wisdom gained through one's own life journey.

The Great Commission, and real discipleship, is a call to fatherhood and motherhood. It is not simply a call to conceive and give birth to new believers. It is a call to disciple, to father, to mother. Paul says, *"I am glad when I suffer for you in my body, for I am participating in the sufferings of Christ that continue for his body, the church"* (Colossians 1:24, NLT). It is a call to both the pains of childbirth and the joys of parenting.

God is mentioned in the Bible many times as being the God of Abraham, Isaac, and Jacob. Over and over, He is referred to as the God of three generations. Not two, four, five, or some other number, but three. Have you ever wondered what is so special about having three generations?

The call of fatherhood goes far beyond the call to be fruitful. If an apple tree produces an incredible amount of apples, it may look like a great success. However, if these apples are not filled with seed which will grow, then this great display of fruitfulness will not bring about multiplication. As mentioned in Matthew 3:10, it is possible to produce bad fruit. *"Even now the ax of God's judgment is poised, ready to sever the roots of the trees. Yes, every tree that does not produce good fruit will be chopped down and thrown into the fire"* (NLT). Our goal cannot simply be to become fruitful, but to be fruitful and multiply. In His instruction on fruitfulness, Jesus says, *"I appointed you to go and produce lasting fruit"* (John 15:16, NLT)

The Great Commission was not just a call to preach the Gospel and win converts. It has to be more than producing spiritual children. It has to be a call to raise fathers and mothers. It is a call to make lasting fruit.

Disciples are the embodiment of lasting fruit. A disciple begins to show maturity when he or she becomes fruitful. Three generations have to be part of our understanding of what we have been called to be. Our success cannot be judged on the second generation, but rather on the third. Fatherhood and motherhood span three generations. It is no accident that the God of three generations is also called Father. Consider this scripture, which speaks about passing on what we have.

> *We will not hide these truths from our*
> *children;*
> *we will tell the next generation*
> *about the glorious deeds of the Lord,*
> *about his power and his mighty wonders.*
> *For he issued his laws to Jacob;*
> *he gave his instructions to Israel.*
> *He commanded our ancestors*
> *to teach them to their children,*
> *so the next generation might know them—*
> *even the children not yet born—*
> *and they in turn will teach their own children.*
> *So each generation should set its hope anew*
> *on God,*
> *not forgetting his glorious miracles*
> *and obeying his commands.*
>
> (Psalm 78:4-7, NLT)

The mindset that says we are to produce converts has to be broken. This is certainly a part of our calling as individuals and as the Church, but it is just a part. We must learn that making disciples means being committed to parenting young believers. For my own children, my goal is not that they just grow up and leave my house one day. My desire for them is that my wife and I are able to teach our sons to be good men, and our daughter to be a good woman, so that they will know how to treat a spouse properly, and that they will learn something from us about how to raise their own kids. Our mission, as parents, has to be to raise good parents. I need to teach my sons how to raise a son.

Part of a father's success is seen in the success of his children, not just in his ability to produce them. Success in discipleship is seen when a disciple becomes mature, and in turn becomes fruitful. We must move people from just being followers, and remaining spiritual infants, to maturity, to leadership. Jesus did call His disciples to follow Him. Then, in time, He left His ministry to them. A parent's true success is seen when their child becomes a father or mother—when it becomes about the God of three generations.

Like those before us, every generation needs to walk in its father's blessing. Throughout the Old Testament, we see the power of a parent's blessing. They would lay their hands on their children and speak into the future generation, as Jacob did in Genesis 49. Lives, directions, and destinies were changed by these blessings, and by the names that were given. It is now up to us, in the Church, to speak this over those into whom we are pouring our lives. This goes beyond speaking positive words over a person. In the natural, we know that words alone can have dramatic effects on a person. There are spiritual principles at work also. Blessing flows from father to son. There is impartation of life, authority, and blessing.

As my own father has prayed and spoken blessing over me, I now pray and speak blessing over my own children. I know that a big part of why, who, and where I am today is because of the upbringing and blessing passed onto me. I now pray that my own children—Matthew, Jordan, and Amanda—will be blessed. I pray that every good thing God has given and imparted to me will rest on them in double proportion or more. I pray that they would experience things in God that I have never experienced, that they would go further, believe for greater things, and that the world would be a different place because they serve God. I also have to pray this over those who I lead, and over this present generation.

> *"For even if you had ten thousand others to teach you about Christ, you have only one spiritual father. For I became your father in Christ Jesus when I preached the Good News to you."*
>
> (1 Corinthians 4:15, NLT)

Paul, in his instruction to Timothy, was by no means putting down the importance of teachers. In fact, they are so necessary that He sets teachers apart as one of the five-fold ministry gifts of the Church. Instead, he was emphasizing the role and importance of another type of relationship, one that began when Paul first preached the Good News to Timothy. Paul becoming Timothy's spiritual father speaks of the importance of not producing spiritual orphans. Timothy immediately experienced not only the spirit of adoption from his Heavenly Father, but also adoption into the family of God through his relationship with Paul.

When the Church focuses only on spiritual birth, we run the risk of producing a generation of orphans. A young group with no one to care for them, feed them, instruct them, protect them, or parent them. If a baby has no one to take care of it, it will die. It is no wonder that a year after most churches do evangelism events or crusades, there are only a small percentage of converts who are still following Christ. We herald our own success, but we are like the tree with lots of seedless apples. It looks really good at first, but all that is left later are the rotten carcasses of fruit that has died.

One of the things Jesus said was that, if you want to be His disciple, you must be willing to take up your cross and follow Him. There certainly is a price to pay to be a disciple, and a father or mother. It involves time, patience, love, a cross, and death to self. It involves us being willing to lay down our lives for Him, and for those we are leading. This is how we know what love really is. A church will only experience long-term growth when it lays down its life to reach, invest, disciple, and parent its own young.

It is also through the process of three generations that we see the importance of each generation. A church without the wisdom of the aged, and the passion of the youth, is dysfunctional. A church without mothers and fathers cannot become truly mature. A church without the young is visionless and lacks passion. This can all start now, but we must be willing to die to ourselves. My prayer is that God would turn our hearts to the children, and that we would be content when our success is seen in those who we are raising up.

15 SONS GO FURTHER

Sons Go Further

Hopefully, you have experienced moments like Jesus did when He looked with compassion on the crowds. I have had moments thinking of my own community and country. While it hasn't happened enough, at times my heart has been broken for the lost and hurting around me.

I know it is the will of the Father that no one would perish. I have wondered what it would take for my entire community to come to a saving knowledge of Christ. I know I have prayed for it. Have you ever wondered what it would look like if it actually happened?

For a true transformation to take place, we would have to see something happen that we have never seen before. My sons, daughter, and disciples would have the opportunity to walk in a different kind of world than I ever did. It would mean that, for my prayer to come true, those after me would have to surpass me. We cannot say that we want worldwide transformation if we cannot desire to be surpassed.

Once we understand the importance of spiritual parents, we need to continue to build on that foundation. There is a huge difference between a father and a teacher. Even Jesus said, in Matthew 10:24, *"Students are not greater than their teacher, and slaves are not greater than their master"* (NLT). As long as we either have an "orphaning" mentality or just think of ourselves as teachers (instead of a father), we are in a losing battle.

Both a father and a teacher want their children or students to succeed. However, a father wants his kids to go further than him. A father wants his children to have a double anointing. A good father is not threatened by the success of his children. He desires it.

If a church today wants to see itself continue to exist, or its community and country changed, it must desire the next generation to go further than it has. This only begins when we begin to view those we are discipling as sons and daughters. When we start desiring that they go further in ministry, reach more people, and go to places where we have never gone, there is a power that is unleashed.

The thought of humbling ourselves and washing the feet of those we are mentoring can be a difficult one, and even an offensive thought. Peter didn't want Jesus to wash his feet, but Jesus had to correct him . He had to live out an example of what we are now to do for each other. Now that my kids have grown, I have to admit that I have no desire to change diapers or clean feces ever again. Before I had children, I didn't want to, either. Although cleaning up after a newborn baby can sound, and actually be, disgusting at times, somehow when you have your own baby, you just do it. Why? Because the child has become a part of you. It is no different with those we lead. When they are family, discipling does not seem burdensome.

The future of many churches today will be determined by when, and if, they can change their view of young people and new believers. To some, they are just a nuisance, too much work, too different, and just too broken to deal with. It would seem it is fine that these people have programs that minister to them, but there is still an "us and them" mentality. We can be guilty of wanting people in our buildings, but they are never truly welcomed into our lives as family.

Sadly, many people are trapped in ministry structures that do not allow for the success of others. Because of the leaders' insecurities, even the thought of someone surpassing them is repulsive. Many ministries have been held back because they face the effects of competition and control. However, this is also bred out of a lack of understanding discipleship and the function of the church as a body. Any spiritual structure simply based on the success of one person will always be a short term endeavour.

As an example, we can look at the stories of two prophets, Elijah and Elisha. It was, in fact, Elisha who received a double anointing of what Elijah had. The Scriptures record almost twice as many miracles under Elisha as under Elijah. In looking at the lives of these two prophets, it would seem that Elisha would be considered the success story.

In the Book of Malachi, it says, *"Look, I am sending you the prophet Elijah before the great and dreadful day of the Lord arrives"* (Malachi 4:5, NLT) Despite the fact that Elisha had a double anointing, and performed twice the miracles, it seems that an honour from God was placed on Elijah, though some may look at him and think he was not as successful. However, in an upside-down kingdom, he is the first.

Elijah, unlike Elisha, had a successor. Not only did Elijah have a successor, but he was even alright with his successor having double the anointing that rested on his own life. Once Elisha received his double anointing, one of the strangest stories in scriptures is recorded. *"Elisha left Jericho and went up to Bethel. As he was walking along the road, a group of boys from the town began mocking and making fun of him. 'Go away, baldy!' they chanted. 'Go away, baldy!' Elisha turned around and looked at them, and he cursed them in the name of the Lord. Then two bears came out of the woods and mauled forty-two of them"* (2 Kings 2:23-24, NLT).

In his lifetime, Elijah did many great things, including blessing the next generation. By investing in another, he ensured that there would be another prophet once he was gone. Elisha, on the other hand, cursed the next generation, and had no successor. There is power in speaking blessing.

I grew up attending charismatic churches, and often heard the following verses spoken. However, for a moment, let's think of who Jesus is speaking to, in the context of the conversation. The scene is set during the last supper, when Jesus is with the disciples. *"Just believe that I am in the Father and the Father is in me. Or at least believe because of the work you have seen me do. I tell you the truth, anyone who believes in me will do the same works I have done, and even greater works, because I am going to be with the Father. You can ask for anything in my name, and I will do it, so that the Son can bring glory to the Father"* (John 14:11-13, NLT).

Most of the teaching I have heard on this passage has focused on miracles, and that "we" will do greater things. However, we may be missing part of Jesus' point. It is true that some of these men sitting with Jesus that night actually did do great things, and arguably even greater things. Many of the disciples travelled much further, and took the Gospel to places Jesus never did. In one setting, on the day of Pentecost, Peter spoke, and three thousand people were added to the church in a day.

Let's focus, though, on the words right before the "greater things" part. *"Anyone who believes in me will do the same works I have done."* In looking at Jesus' life with these men, I have often wondered how they would have interpreted these words. Early on, Jesus washed His disciples feet, and then told them to do the same. If they had looked at everything Jesus had done in the past three years, perhaps they would have taken it to mean, "Everything Jesus did, we must go do." This, of course, seems like the obvious answer, but look at it through the eyes of discipleship. If Jesus focused on developing these individuals, then wouldn't they have to do the same for others?

The statement ends with the words, *"so that the Son can bring glory to the Father."* Later in the same setting, Jesus also says, *"When you produce much fruit, you are my true disciples. This brings great glory to my Father"* (John 15:8, NLT). At least part, if not all, of what Jesus is referring to is discipleship and fruitfulness, because that is what brings glory to the Father.

And could there be more? When I think of the desire of a father for his children, I am overwhelmed to see the Father's heart being revealed through His son, Jesus. Was it His desire for these men to go further than Him? I believe we are seeing in Jesus a father's heart for His spiritual children. He discipled them up to surpass even Him in the works they did.

When we take on a discipleship and fathering mentality, it changes our motivations. It takes us past simply wanting to have new people in our churches. We not only want to see people come to know Christ… we want them to succeed. We want them to grow. We want them to become fruitful. We want to see our sons and daughters go further.

SPIRIT OF ADOPTION -
THE END OR ORPHANS

Spirit of Adoption— The End of Orphans

One of the biggest weakness in our churches is real follow-up and integration. The western Church spends an incredible amount of time, money, and resources on outreach events, yet there is very little growth to show for it. While many churches try their hardest to have an open door, the majority of people who come visit, or even respond to salvation calls, do not become active church members.

Once we begin to understand the need for spiritual mothers and fathers, we must take the next step. Seeing the need does not mean the need is being met. At some point, the family of God needs to learn to adopt new members. Adoption goes beyond the superficial. It is more than a handshake or greeting once a week. It is an invitation to become part of a family.

There is a huge difference between being welcoming and having a spirit of adoption. Churches can go out of their way to make people at ease, which is actually a huge help. However, we use church buildings as a place to invite people without having to get personally involved. Church attendance alone does not make mature disciples. So unless real connections are made, we are limiting growth, and limiting our future.

This is not a small or big church issue. In fact, all of the largest churches in the world are based on small group models. It is true that you can get lost in a crowd. Once groups of any kind get too large, it is hard to deal with individuals on a personal basis. This could be why, in His wisdom, Jesus only chose twelve disciples.

Small groups or churches, however, sometimes actually have a harder time letting new people into their family than their larger counterparts. Once a core develops, it is often hard to let a new person or family in, because it means change, and change is usually painful. Adoption means making room for new family members. It can be awkward at first, but in time it becomes natural. But most new people never it make it that far.

Smaller groups or churches sometimes think they are more welcoming, because they are small and therefore more intimate. However, have you ever walked in on someone being intimate, or had someone walk in on you? There is nothing welcoming or comfortable about that; it is only awkward. Adoption is not about the size of the group, but rather the attitude and philosophy.

As individuals, it is actually possible for us to hide from discipleship within the programs of the church. These programs can serve as a way for us to express our faith without ever really getting involved in the lives of others. Now, people operate in many different areas of gifting, which put us all in different roles, and I am not saying that many of these ministries are not needed. However, we can be so busy doing good things that we do not have time to disciple anyone personally. Also, just because we are gifted in something does not exclude us from discipleship. If you are a great singer, for example, but have decided you don't have to pour into anyone else, you probably should not be leading in worship.

We can be caught up in trying to do so much evangelism or planting seed that we neglect to water and care for the seed so that it can grow. Most people want to be involved in procreation, but not everyone wants to change the diapers. Yet if we are to see lasting fruit, it is always going to be a little messy. New babies need time to mature, to grow, to bond, to ask questions, to observe, and to learn. Those are their needs, but it takes an adoption into a family for those needs to actually be met.

A church of any size is not just a gathering of people. A church is supposed to be a covenant community, a community that has committed itself to the growth and protection of all its members. Discipleship is only truly effective in covenant. It is when we understand that we actually have a commitment to another person that many scriptures really take on their intended meaning. We are not simply called to attend meetings with other people. We are told that there are things we must do for each other. These things usually do not happen unless it is within a covenant or a discipleship relationship.

If we are going to understand what adoption means, here are just a few scriptures that paint the picture for us.

The cornerstone of all the following verses is love. In fact, Jesus said that love would be the biggest sign that we are in fact His disciples. *"Your love for one another will prove to the world that you are my disciples"* (John 13:35, NLT) This is not an option for anyone wanting to disciple others. In fact, it is a command. *"Love means doing what God has commanded us, and he has commanded us to love one another, just as you heard from the beginning"* (2 John 1:6, NLT)

This love for one another is needed if we are going to be able to call those we are discipling "friends," like Jesus did. Love is also needed if we are going to enter into covenant and discipleship with pure motivations.

In the Book of First Samuel, we read about a story of David and Jonathan. Jonathan was the young man who would become king, and the son of the present king, Saul. His father, Saul, was trying to kill David.

"After David had finished talking with Saul, he met Jonathan, the king's son. There was an immediate bond between

them, for Jonathan loved David... And Jonathan made a solemn pact with David, because he loved him as he loved himself" (1 Samuel, 18:1,3, NLT) True covenants are birthed in love. Jonathan vowed to try and keep David from harm so he could go wherever God was calling him, even if it would mean, one day, David would be king instead of him. This is where the love for those we are pouring into should bring us.

There is no substitute for actually spending time with other people. In the Book of Acts, at the beginning of the church, we get a picture of the lives of the first believers. *"They worshiped together at the Temple each day, met in homes for the Lord's Supper, and shared their meals with great joy and generosity—all the while praising God and enjoying the goodwill of all the people. And each day the Lord added to their fellowship those who were being saved"* (Acts 2:46-47, NLT) There was certainly a personal connection between this group of believers. They not only met in the temple, but they would go and spend time in each other's homes.

In Hebrews, we are again reminded of the importance of being together. *"And let us not neglect our meeting together, as some people do, but encourage one another, especially now that the day of his return is drawing near"* (Hebrews 10:25, NLT) While this verse has been used to back up the importance of attending services, that may be taking it a bit out of context. If you look at where most of the early Christians met with each other, you will learn that the majority of their time was spent together in each other's homes. It was here that people ate together, shared together, grew together, discussed together, and became family.

Spending time in corporate worship and teaching is a very healthy expression of our faith, but it is not to be our only one. The question we have to ask ourselves is, is there a place where you are connecting with others, a place you can ask questions, a place where you can pour into others, and others can pour into you, a place that is so safe that you could do the following? *"Confess your sins to each other and pray for each other so that you may be healed. The earnest prayer of a righteous person has great power and produces wonderful results"* (James 5:16, NLT)

When we do not have a place where things like this can happen, we actually rob people of the healing and growth that occurs when confession, and then forgiveness, takes place. *"Make allowance for each other's faults, and forgive anyone who offends you. Remember, the Lord forgave you, so you must forgive others"* (Colossians 3:13, NLT) It is quite amazing how a family accepts the imperfections and uniqueness of its own members. When there are shortcomings, a family does not somehow stop being a family. Family does what this verse says. We really do *"make allowance for each other's faults."* This is particularly good news because even leaders, and those discipling, are not perfect, and we need acceptance and forgiveness just as often.

We also need to make sure that people do not give up when they are faced with doubts, circumstances, failings, or just the busyness of life. 1 Thessalonians 5:11 says, *"So encourage each other and build each other up, just as you are already doing"* (NLT). Your words of life can be the very thing that keeps people from falling back into death. Practice encouragement. In fact, push people forward. Hebrews 10:24 says, *"Let us think of ways to motivate one another to acts of love and good works"* (NLT). As someone who is discipling, you have to be the chief motivator and cheerleader for those God puts in your path.

When there is failure among family, we do not simply throw our family members out. Families take care of their wounded and sick. We help bring them back to health. In the same way, we need to do this for those who we are discipling. *"Dear brothers and sisters, if another believer is overcome by some sin, you who are godly should gently and humbly help that person back onto the right path. And be careful not to fall into the same temptation yourself. Share each other's burdens, and in this way obey the law of Christ"* (Galatians 6:1-2, NLT). The things that hinder and burden us down are to be shared, and together we can overcome them.

When we talk about adopting people into our lives, we realize that these are just a few of the actions the Scriptures instruct us to do for them and others. These are the some of the ways we can use what God has given us to bless others. *"God has given each of you a gift from his great variety of spiritual gifts. Use them well to serve one another"* (1 Peter 4:10, NLT). When we adopt people into our lives, we are taking a reasonable responsibility for them. People still have their own free will—we can only be responsible for our own decisions to do the right thing. People still make their own choices. Even Jesus had disciples who betrayed and denied him, so you cannot put an unreasonable pressure on yourself to assume that all will stay.

The question we are left with is, are we willing to let the spirit of adoption work in our lives, ministries, and churches? Are we ready to let people into our lives? Are we ready to love and serve? Are we ready for new family members?

IDEA

Where Do I Start?

This book may be calling you to a journey, and of course you may be asking, *Who do I start with?* Well, how about starting at home?

I have been asked many times if we are supposed to have lifetime disciples. I am not sure if there is a clear answer to this. I do have a high respect for many of the churches or models that use this approach. I do believe that God has or will give you some lifelong disciples, though. These are our own children.

We need to remember to speak the blessings we speak on others onto them. We need to ensure that the time we spend with others cannot take us away from the time we need to spend with our own families. I have had three teenagers growing up in my house at once, and while many days I did not feel they were all blessings from God, they really are. I may have other people in my life that I pour into for a time, and perhaps some for much of my life, but my children are my first lifelong disciples.

What lessons have we taught our children this week or month? Why not do something together that will cause them to see you living out what you say? Instead of sending them off to a soup kitchen or a mission trip, you need to go with them. Let them see you help someone out. Do ministry together. Pass it on.

SECTION
FOUR

17 THE TRANSFORMATION - LIFE IN THE SPIRIT

The Transformation— Life in the Spirit

When thinking about bringing in the harvest, one word comes to our minds before any other: Work. As mentioned earlier, thinking about winning and discipling the harvest can seem daunting and overwhelming. When we hear a challenge to win our friends, co-workers, and family to the Lord, the first reaction is to cringe at the mere thought of it. It is not that we don't desire for everyone to come to a saving knowledge of Christ, we just don't know how it is ever going to happen in our lifetime.

During a service many years ago, I heard a story about how we should bring in the harvest. The speaker shared about a dream, or picture, he had of a beautiful bride, which represented the Church. In his story, the bride was dressed in her gown, dancing in a field of grain. This dancing bride was anticipating the coming of her groom. In her hands, she was holding a sickle. As she danced and spun, the grain was being cut all around her. It was not a burdensome task, but rather the harvest was being swept up in the celebration that was taking place.

It was a very different idea from the one most of us have about harvesting. However, it may be more correct than many of our own preconceptions. In Acts 1:8, it says, *"But you will receive power when the Holy Spirit comes upon you. And you will be my witnesses, telling people about me everywhere—in Jerusalem, throughout Judea, in Samaria, and to the ends of the earth"* (NLT). Our first reaction to hearing these words may be that we need to rush out and just start talking to everyone. It is true that we are going to have to speak, because, *"faith comes from hearing, that is, hearing the Good News about Christ"* (Romans 10:17, NLT) However, rushing into the fields may not be the first step we need to take.

We have to make sure that we do not miss what Jesus is saying. He did not say that you would go everywhere and witness. He says that you will *be* a witness. This speaks to something much deeper than just an action to be performed. This speaks of something we are to become, an inward transformation caused by the work of the Holy Spirit. Witnessing, or telling others about Him, is a direct result of this work. In the gospels, Jesus mentions several things we are to do, but many times He also states things we are to *be*.

For example, in Matthew 5:13-14, He says, *"You are the salt of the earth. But if the salt loses its saltiness, how can it be made salty again? It is no longer good for anything, except to be thrown out and trampled by men. You are the light of the world. A city on a hill cannot be hidden"* (NIV). He says "you are" both salt and light. Unlike some of the teaching I have heard on this scripture, it does not state that we are simply reflecting God's light. Rather, Jesus in fact says, "You are the light." Of course, our first thought is that Jesus is the Light of the world, so we can't be. However, we cannot change what Jesus said to fit our own theology.

These scriptures all point to something that happens within us, that we are to *be* something, and not just focus on the work we have to do. It also shows our incredible need to let God work on us, to be changed into His likeness. Though speaking, sharing, and witnessing has to happen, it is not the starting point.

In Acts 1:4-5, we read Jesus' own instructions to the disciples. *"Once when he was eating with them, he commanded them, 'Do not leave Jerusalem until the Father sends you the gift he promised, as I told you before. John baptized with water, but in just a few days you will be baptized with the Holy Spirit"* (NLT). After the outpouring of the Holy Spirit that is recorded in Acts 2, we see the incredible transformation that takes place in the lives of the disciples. We see a group of people who, before their relationship with Christ, were doubters, deniers, and sceptics. All became bold witnesses for Christ. Peter, who had denied Jesus when asked if he knew Him, now was standing up proclaiming the Good News to some of the same people who had taken part in crucifying Jesus.

There are some things I truly enjoy in life. I have been an extreme sport fanatic since I was young. I don't want to date myself, but I was among one of the first snowboarders allowed on our local ski hill. I still remember having to do a test to prove it was possible to even turn and stop on a snowboard, because no one had ever done that on the mountain before. I have skateboarded for over twenty years, mountain biked, mountain climbed, and have found lots of other ways to injure myself. When it is warm, my main source of transportation is my motorcycle. I have hardly missed a single pay-per view UFC event in years. However, I also enjoy a few quieter hobbies. I love to sit by our fire-place playing my acoustic guitar with no one around.

While these may or may not be your favourite things, they are mine. If you want to get me talking, just mention them to me. Whether we have been friends for years, or have just met, you will hear all kinds of stories. You won't have to force any of this conversation out of me. Why? Because I am like everyone else. We all talk about what brings us enjoyment. Ever try to shut up a football, hockey, or baseball fan when their team is playing, or especially when they are winning?

There is a huge need for us to know what we believe and why. Paul gave Timothy this instruction: *"Work hard so you can present yourself to God and receive his approval.*

Be a good worker, one who does not need to be ashamed and who correctly explains the word of truth" (2 Timothy 2:15, NLT). Also, the Apostle Peter gave a similar teaching, *"Instead, you must worship Christ as Lord of your life. And if someone asks about your Christian hope, always be ready to explain it"* (1 Peter 3:15, NLT). There is no substitute for knowing why and what you believe.

This knowledge does not mean that witnessing must become a set formula that we are to repeat to everyone we meet. I do not mean to put down any ministry that uses certain tools, as God has used many different means to speak to people throughout history. In fact, the Holy Spirit is very creative and will give people ideas, plans, dreams, and visions of things to do and say.

It is possible for you to witness (speak) without being transformed. However, it is impossible for you to be transformed, to be salt and light, and not share it with anyone. When what we do comes out of who we are, it goes past reciting a formula; it comes from within our hearts.

In Luke 6:45, we read where our words are to come from. *"A good person produces good things from the treasury of a good heart, and an evil person produces evil things from the treasury of an evil heart. What you say flows from what is in your heart"* (NLT). Before we speak, we must make sure there is something happening in our hearts. Is there compassion? Is there love? Are we hearing where God is telling us to go?

One of the most powerful tools we have to reach others is our testimony. This is not just the story about how we came to God. Our testimony includes that part, but our complete testimony is the story of how God is working today. It is how, despite our failings, we keep our trust in Him. It is our present experiences, the good, and the bad. It is our life. It is not just about the things God saved you from, but also about all the incredible things God has saved us for.

Along with my own passions in life that I love to talk about, I have a few more. Every year, I take time to serve others in third-world countries. I am presently helping to start a youth centre in my own town. I have found that these passions keep me talking about what God is doing today, because I am presently involved with them. Our testimony evolves as we live our lives.

If we truly talk about what brings us enjoyment, we need to let our hearts be filled with the right things. Psalm 37:4 tells us where to begin: *"Take delight in the Lord, and he will give you your heart's desires"* (NLT). If we want the overflow of our mouths to speak about the things of God, we have to have Him as our focus. We have to ask ourselves, *Where is my joy found?* In Psalm 16:11, we read where, as believers, it should be found. *"You have made known to me the path of life; you will fill me with joy in your presence, with eternal pleasures at your right hand"* (NIV).

It is in the presence of God that we find our joy. When we are filled with His presence, which is what Jesus told His disciples to wait for in Acts 1, we change. We become something we weren't before. The task at hand does not seem quite as overwhelming, because we have something we did not have before, something that is rooted in the joy of the Lord. *"Don't be dejected and sad, for the joy of the Lord is your strength!"* (Nehemiah 8:10, NLT)

This is not a journey that we have to take on our own. We are taking on this journey of discipleship with others, but also with the Holy Spirit. We need to be prepared, but first we need to be transformed. The starting point is learning to be witnesses. One of the roles the Holy Spirit has is to point people to Jesus. Imagine what can happen when you team up with God. When we stop trying to do it on our own, our joy and strength will come from Him.

IDEA

Overflow

Over the years, I have struggled at times with what to share with my church. Yet sometimes I have a hard time narrowing it down, because I have too much to share. I have discovered, by going through both types of seasons, that many times there is a reason why I am there.

When I am putting good things into my mind and life, I don't struggle with having to come up with ideas and messages. If you want to have something to pour into others, you must decide to be a person who receives. It goes beyond just having a teachable spirit. You need to be intentionally putting good things into your mind and spirit.

Here are a few suggestions. Read books. Put the teachings of great men and women of God into your mind. Listen to good preaching. There are endless messages recorded that you can listen to on podcasts, webcasts, and television. Spend time in silence, listening to what He has to say to you and for those around you.

We need to have words of life to pass on. If you want to lead, you need to become a conduit of His power, grace, mercy, truth, light, and presence. Always remember: *"A good person produces good things from the treasury of a good heart, and an evil person produces evil things from the treasury of an evil heart. What you say flows from what is in your heart"* (Luke 6:45, NLT)

Make sure your heart if full and overflowing.

18 THE BEGINNING - LIFE

The Beginning—Life

I t is God's will that no one would miss out on the life that He offers to us. It was His love for this broken world that caused Him to send His son, Jesus, to die on a cross and bring salvation to everyone who believes. We have been called to be His representatives, to share this Good News with those who have never heard, to make disciples, to baptize them, and to teach them everything He has passed onto us.

When Jesus looked upon the crowds and had compassion on them, His instructions were simple. Pray for labourers. This message is also for our generation today. Pray that the Lord of the Harvest would raise up and send labourers. Pray that God would indeed wake us up to see what is around us. Pray that He would break our hearts to a point that we have to put away our old ways so that we now can live in a new way.

One day, after Jesus spoke to the woman at the well, His disciples found Him, and they had this conversation.

> Meanwhile, the disciples were urging Jesus, "Rabbi, eat something."
>
> But Jesus replied, "I have a kind of food you know nothing about."
>
> "Did someone bring him food while we were gone?" the disciples asked each other.
>
> Then Jesus explained: "My nourishment comes from doing the will of God, who sent me, and from finishing his work. You know the saying, 'Four months between planting and harvest.' But I say, wake up and look around. The fields are already ripe for harvest."
>
> (John 4:31-35, NLT)

Today, we once again need to see discipleship and maturity come to the Body of Christ. We have been called to minister to this generation. Many churches are struggling to reach the masses because they really have no plan or process to reach and grow the masses. For most believers, city-wide transformation is just a dream. We may hope and pray for it, but we don't really expect it to ever happen.

This, however, is our call. We, like Jesus, need to take up the call to be sent ones. We need to be able to say that doing the will of the Father makes us who we are. This is our nourishment. This is our life. This is what we will be about. We will set out to walk in His footsteps, to follow His voice, and to continue His mission.

"Jesus told him, 'I am the way, the truth, and the life. No one can come to the Father except through me'" (John 14:6, NLT) Real life is living in Christ, living for His purposes, living in fellowship, being the Body. It is fulfilling His purposes of seeking and saving the lost, and bringing glory to the Father. There is nothing that brings more contentment in life than giving yourself to following the voice and heart of God. Everything we do comes into perfect alignment with who God created us to be. All the talents, abilities, personality, giftings, and unique things about us come together to bring glory to Him.

If you are bored or disillusioned with your Christian walk, be set free to do what you were created for. *"For we are God's workmanship, created in Christ Jesus to do good works, which God prepared in advance for us to do"* (Ephesians 2:10, NIV) You have been made, and are called, to be fruitful and multiply.

If doing the will of the Father is Jesus' goal, then as those who are His followers we must embrace the same. Imagine this same calling being on your life. As Jesus began His ministry, He read this scripture in the synagogue: *"The scroll of Isaiah the prophet was handed to him. He unrolled the scroll and found the place where this was written: 'The Spirit of the Lord is upon me, for he has anointed me to*

*bring Good News to the poor. He has sent me to proclaim
that captives will be released, that the blind will see, that the
oppressed will be set free, and that the time of the Lord's
favor has come'"* (Luke 4:17-19, NLT) Christ gave us this
mission to continue. The Holy Spirit anoints, and empowers
us to do the work. We have a message to proclaim. It may
seem like foolishness to many, but it is Good News, the
words that bring life.

Discipleship is patience and persistence. It is putting
aside our own attempts at personal greatness and dedicat-
ing our lives solely to the purposes of Christ. It is investing in
today, and knowing it will multiply tomorrow. It is sowing
the seeds that will bring in a great harvest. How incredible it
would be if our lives could be like that of the good soil mentioned in Matthew 13:23: *"The seed that fell on good soil
represents those who truly hear and understand God's
word and produce a harvest of thirty, sixty, or even a hundred times as much as had been planted!"* (NLT) We would
truly hear and understand the voice of the Shepherd leading us.

This is something you are not just going to tell others.
This is something people need to see you live out. The days
of challenging people, but never walking with them, are
over. Discipleship is real. It is a calling to a new life, a new
way, a new purpose. It is death to our old ways. It will sepa-
rate you from the ordinary, but God has not called you to
the ordinary. He has called you to be like Him. He has called
you to *"go and make disciples of all the nations, baptizing*

them in the name of the Father and the Son and the Holy Spirit. Teach these new disciples to obey all the commands I have given you. And be sure of this: I am with you always, even to the end of the age" (Matthew 28:19-20, NLT).

CPSIA information can be obtained at www.ICGtesting.com
Printed in the USA
LVOW10s1010240913

353746LV00006B/24/P